THE WEE GUIDE TO
SCOTTISH WOMEN

(the good, the bad and the gallus)

Deedee Cuddihy

ISBN 978 0 9930986 2 8

Published by Deedee Cuddihy
10 Otago Street,
Glasgow G12 8JH
Scotland

Cover design: Anonymous (Glasgow)
Ltd.

Printed by Bell and Bain Ltd,
Glasgow

Dedication

This modest publication is dedicated to Iain Scott whose own first book got me started on mine; to members of Merchant Voices and Pat Woods' book group at Hillhead Library; to Caryl Godwin and to Leslie and Blackie for help with the title. And a big thanks to the two lovely women who appear on the front cover, for letting me take their picture.

Note on photographs: *None of the women who kindly let me use photographs of them for this book are bad (to my knowledge!) but they are all gallus - and born in Scotland.*

Ma maw's a millionaire

Blue eyes and curly hair

See her walkin doon the street

Wi her big banana feet

Ma maw's a millionaire

My mother was tone deaf but that didn't stop her singing "California Here I Come" at the top of her voice at family gatherings. Another of her party pieces was performing a handstand against the wall with her skirt tucked into her pants. That was really embarrassing.

(Charlie)

I'm a bit hazy about everything that happened at my nephew's wedding but I do remember falling into a flower bed on the way out of the reception venue. Ah, alcohol!

(Sheena, from an email)

Pubs in my area of Glasgow were more fun in the late 1970s, especially if Mary was around. She'd been a life model at the art school and, at the weekends, when last orders had been called, she and her pal would regularly finish the night by stripping off their tops and bras and flinging them at each other across the bar, to the applause of the rest of the customers. I think she went on to train as a primary school teacher.

(Mary Ann)

My aunt Maisie had really splashed out one Christmas and booked the family a box at the pantomime. She was quite well-oiled by the time we got to the theatre - as was normal for her on these occasions - and made a big show of opening a box of Maltesers to pass around. Then, as the orchestra was warming up, she leaned over the balcony parapet to get a closer look, causing the Maltesers to tip out of their box and cascade down noisily on to the drums. At this, the audience looked up, Maisie waved at them extravagantly and they waved back, apparently under the impression that she was part of the show. We, of course, were mortified.

(Les)

My younger sister has always been a bit of a show-off. If the weather's good, she loves going for a run in her white Volkswagen Golf Cabriolet with the top down and her blonde hair blowing in the wind. And why not? She's a widow and in her late 60s so she can do what she wants. I call her a poseur but it's only family banter.

(Hugh, church elder)

I was in hospital, overdue with my first baby, when I met a girl in the patients' lounge who was in the same situation. She'd heard lots of horror stories and was very nervous about going into labour. I was feeling very confident because I'd been to NCT classes so I did my best to calm her fears. As it turned out, I had an extremely painful time and screamed the place down. In the lounge the next day, I met the same girl who was all smiles this time, thanked me for my encouraging words and told me that the birth had, as predicted by me, been fine. "But did you hear the terrible noise that other poor woman was making?" she asked. I paused for just a second before replying: "Yes - I heard her, too."

(Penny)

THE WEE GUIDE TO
« SCOTTISH WOMEN »

Email sent by the author to Nicola Sturgeon in January, 2014 (before she became First Minister):

Dear Ms. Sturgeon,

I hesitate to contact you on an issue that seems, on the face of it, relatively unimportant. However, my husband and I have almost come to blows over the question of how tall you are. He claims he saw you some years ago in Queen Street station and that you were "about five feet tall." I have rubbished his claim, saying that it can't have been you because you are probably around 5'5" - possibly taller.

I hope you can help - especially if you are, in fact, not as tiny as my husband claims. If you are, then I probably won't tell him.

Yours sincerely,

Deedee Cuddihy

Hi
Thanks for your email! I am around 5'4". I'll
leave it to you to decide whether or not to
come clean with your husband!
Kind regards
Nicola

Nicola Sturgeon MSP
Glasgow Southside

"The wheels are back on the wagon - and I'm the nag hitched up to tow it."

Annabel Goldie (now Baroness Goldie), after being named as the new leader of the Scottish Conservatives, back in 2005.

I got a job in a biscuit factory when I left school - I was so young I was still wearing ankle socks! - and the woman in charge of the recipe room I worked in was called Vera Love who was so proper and lady-like that if you needed to go to the toilet, you weren't allowed to use the word "toilet" and you certainly didn't say bog or cludgie or kazi; you had to call it "the bathroom".

(Frances)

The ladies of a Scottish bowling club have thrown in their aprons in a row over making tea for the male members. If the duties are not shared amongst all the members, male and female, of Broughty Castle club, they will stop altogether. Betty Baxter, 73, the women's president, said: "We are being treated as second-class citizens but that's what some men do, is it not?"

(from The Herald)

I started my training as a librarian in Glasgow under Olivia Scott who was head of Shettleston Library at the time. She was maybe seen as a bit eccentric but she was fantastic to work for. Another lad was starting out at the same time as me and one of our daily jobs was to make Olivia her cup of tea. She had very high standards and we had to lay out a table cloth and use a china tea pot - with just the exact amount of tea in it - and a china cup and saucer plus a sugar basin and milk jug. But she was also the person who collected our union dues.

(Patrick)

A Newton Mearns woman has avoided a prison sentence after she admitted putting dog faeces in her husband's curry – and laughing when he started eating it. The 47-year-old pled guilty to culpable and reckless conduct but Sheriff Susan Sinclair discharged her without punishment, after learning that the woman had suffered years of mental cruelty.

(from a news report)

My mom's parents are Scottish and although she doesn't have an accent, she does have a red face, a nasty temper, likes to drink, play golf and have a good time - like any other true Scotsman!

(American film maker Mack Palhemys)

Scottish women are tough – but in a good way. And they work harder than Scottish men.

(Ricardo, from Spain)

A small word of warning: if you are searching for single Scottish women for marriage because you have some pre-conceived idea about what Scottish ladies are like, bear in mind that modern Scottish women may be very different from any stereotypes you might have. If you are a Scottish man, you probably already know this.

(from an internet dating site)

What has surprised me since coming to Scotland from Cameroon is seeing a man hitting a woman in the street. Even more surprising is seeing a woman hitting a man. You would rarely get that in Cameroon; women are more respectful there – at least in public.

(Charles)

Ma maw's a millionaire

Blue eyes and curly hair

Stoats ma faither aff the
wa,

Like a wee cahochie baw.

Ma Maw's a millionaire

A *"shirriking"* was a word used in Glasgow to describe a public dressing down, usually done by a women to a man. If a husband decided to stray with a "fancy wumman" or punctuate an argument with his hands, or spend too much time in the pub or the bookies, his aggrieved spouse would meet him at the close mouth (of the tenement) and publicly explain to the neighbours exactly what the aberrant behaviour was - and always at the top of her lungs. The reason for this was safety because if a Glasgow male "lifted his haun" in public to his wife, the rest of the female neighbours would quickly emasculate him!

(thanks to Jean)

I'm from North Carolina in the United States and knew nothing about Glasgow when I applied for a job at the university, 25 years ago. However, a female colleague from Manchester warned me: "Stay away from the tough Glaswegian women." I ended up marrying one!

(Will)

My first serious girlfriend turned out to be a bit of a psycho. Only about a month into the relationship, she suggested we move in together and start thinking about having children. This really alarmed me so I said: "Look, this just isn't working" and broke it off. That didn't go down well with her and, over the next few months, she sent me a letter every week - in the days before emails and texts - which was always sprayed with perfume and said the same thing: " You b******, you've ruined my life. I hope you're proud of yourself."

(Iain)

Over three-quarters of Scottish women say they've had a multiple orgasm, more than women elsewhere in the UK, according to a sex survey.

I'm 60 and my current partner is much younger so when I told a friend that my son and his wife were expecting their first baby, she asked: "How's Stephen going to feel about sleeping with a granny?" and I said: "Well, he's been sleeping with a pensioner for almost a year and there've been no complaints."

(Sandra)

My parents divorced when I was very young and although my mum never lived with another man again, she had a number of boyfriends over the years. I'd forgotten just how many until her funeral, when they all appeared - alongside my father - and queued up at the end of the service to shake my hand and offer their condolences. I had a real struggle trying to remember their names!

(Jenny)

New technology held no fears for Margaret in her later years. And the large print facility on her Kindle meant that, despite failing eyesight, she was able to enjoy reading "50 Shades of Grey."

(from a eulogy at a Lanarkshire funeral)

When I got married in the 1950s, weddings were nothing like as elaborate as they are now. It was mostly just close family and we had the ceremony and then a nice meal, followed by an evening at the theatre. My mother had bought tickets for the musical comedy "And So To Bed" and I don't remember anyone at the time remarking how embarrassingly appropriate it was to the occasion!

(Chrissie)

We knew so little about sex when I was a teenager that when the older girls at school told us you could get pregnant if a boy put his tongue in your mouth, we believed them.

(Anna)

A Pope who visited Scotland more than 500 years ago found the women "good-looking and comely." But he disapproved of their moral character - especially their "lavish distribution of kisses".

I don't know if it's still the same but when you travelled overnight on the train in Italy, you'd get a berth in a mixed compartment, male and female. I was abroad on my own and it was just me and a Catholic priest in the compartment by ourselves. I was single and he was young and good looking so I ended up getting off with him.

(Carla)

A Scottish woman thought to be Britain's oldest virgin has celebrated her 105th birthday - and said the secret to long life is celibacy. The retired secretary who was born in Glasgow, said: "People have asked me if I am a homosexual and the answer is no. I have just never been interested in sex. I imagine there is a lot of hassle involved and I have always been busy doing other things."

(from The Herald)

I've been married for over 20 years and I've never had an orgasm.

(Margaret)

"My mum better stop asking me if I got a 'lumber' after a night out"

(a Scottish tweeter)

"my mum jus said she would pay someone to go out with me....don't think it could get much worse"

(a Scottish tweeter)

"Told my mum its a guy interviewing me tomorrow and she goes " unbutton your shirt 2 more than usual, show him what you bring to the table" !"

(a Scottish tweeter)

When I was in third year at a Catholic high school, our form teacher, Miss McKee was always telling the class: "Every time a girl kisses a boy, Our Lady cries in Heaven."

(Paul)

"You can start asking questions, Kenneth, when you bring a decent bag to school!"

(comedian Karen Dunbar's school teacher character on "Chewin' the Fat")

I had remained friends with a woman I taught with at one time, who was much older than I and had always been considered "eccentric" but was becoming more so, and I took my granddaughter with me one day to visit her. Like any normal three-year-old, she started exploring the room we were sitting in and suddenly my friend glared at her and said, in a very imperious voice: "Has no one ever told you it's rude to look in other people's cupboards?"

(Laura)

We were having an inspection in the high school I taught in and one of the HMI team was in my classroom. After I'd taken the register, one of the pupils, Sharon, piped up and said: "Sir, I've split ma trousers." So I told her to take them along to the Home Economics department to get them sorted, and turned back to the lesson I was teaching. A few moments later, there was a cough from the Inspector and I looked up to see Sharon actually taking her trousers off. I shouted at her: "I meant take the trousers along to Home Economics with you in them!"

(Richard)

My mother is in her late 80s but she's still fit enough to manage a 3Fs wash every morning at the bathroom sink. That stands for Face, Fanny and Feet.

(Brenda)

A woman who is believed to be the world's oldest yoga teacher has vowed to continue holding her popular classes after her 100th birthday. Mrs Dennison, from Fife, recently suffered a fall but the nonagenarian – who has held weekly sessions for pensioners in Dunfermline for the past 40 years – has promised to fight back to full fitness for the new term.

(from a news report)

Yer maw's so old she co-wrote the ten commandments.

(www.urbandictionary.com)

My grannie is really nice and there's nothing wrong with her mental health but when she's talking about a friend whose memory is going, she'll say that so-and-so has "got the dimension."

(Lorna)

We were having lunch at my aunt and uncle's house, only a few weeks after the Boxing Day tsunami in Thailand, and my aunt said: "Wasn't it terrible about all those people dying in that tiramisu?" It took us a few moments to realise what she was referring to.

(Alison)

Two very superstitious women from Kintyre were in Glasgow for the day and revealed how exhausting shopping in the city can be, due to the many entrances and exits to be found in department stores, and the necessity for superstitious people like themselves to enter and leave a building by the same door.

(Kate)

I had a pal whose granny lived with them and one day when I was over there, we noticed her gran was wearing her dress inside out. My pal thought maybe it was because she was becoming confused but when she told her, her gran said: "I did notice I had put it on inside out but I couldn't put it right without taking it off and starting again and it's bad luck to do that, so I'm stuck with it for the rest of the day."

(woman on the bus to Largs)

Scottish women are the slimmest in the UK, despite the fact that they drink more alcohol and eat more chocolate than women south of the border, according to a health survey.

"Made my mum a bacon, sausage and tattie scone sandwich and she said "make sure you use that low-fat butter"."

(a Scottish tweeter)

My aunt was short and round and was never known to move faster than was necessary. I was spending my school holidays with her in Fife and while she was walking me to the bus stop to go back up to Dundee, she suddenly broke into a run - something I'd never seen her do before - and headed straight across the street to the baker's. It turned out that icing sugar had come off ration and there were French Fancies in the window and she was determined to get some.

(Helen)

I used to love being in the kitchen when my mother was baking because she'd give me butter balls to eat. They were, literally, bits of butter, rolled into balls, and dipped in white sugar."

(Alistair)

"I'm just going to leave this here."

(Scottish Labour leader, Kezia Dugdale captions a twitter pic of her homemade strawberry and chocolate cake, in a bid to attract new members to the party.)

I went to live with my grannie after my parents died. She was a real "waste not, want not" person and when I started going out to work, she'd make up my sandwiches using anything that was left over from dinner the night before including things like chicken curry which was both weird and embarrassing.

(actor and musician Billy Boyd,
interviewed by Edie Stark)

My granny used to make tripe boiled in milk with onions. We children called it "wet nappies" and everyone in the family hated it, except my father. When she was going to make it, my granny would phone my mother and my father would go round there for tea.

(Robyn)

"My cooking is so bad, the kids call Child Line when I come into the kitchen."

(Comedian Susan Morrison)

"Fillet of a fenny snake,
   In the caldron boil and bake;
   Eye of newt, and toe of frog,
   Wool of bat, and tongue of dog,
   Adder's fork, and blind-worm's sting,
   Lizard's leg, and owlet's wing."

(Scottish women cooking up a storm -
literally - in Shakespeare's famous play,
Macbeth)

When she was older, I used to go shopping for my Paisley granny on a Saturday morning. I had a long list and several shops to go to. You had to buy some things in the Co-op, some things in the "Maypole" grocers, others in the butcher's, the baker, the veg shop and so on. It took hours. Woe betide you if you tried to buy things in the wrong shop, as she always knew! I was paid one shilling for this.

(Christine)

I trained my children to help with the housework as soon as they were old enough to load the washing machine. I had to because I went out to work every day and I didn't want to come back to a messy house. Fast forward to the next generation and I noticed my grandson, when he was about three, standing at the window one day, rubbing a circle of condensation off so he could see out. I said: "Hold on a minute" and went and got him a cloth so he could give the glass a proper clean!

(Angela)

"FACT: Scottish women are the only people in the world who talk about good weather in terms of how much washing they could get done. Even in Cancun they are like: *"aww how good would it be to be able to get the weans bedsheets out in this?"*"

(a Scottish tweeter)

I have a friend who believes in doing the bare minimum when it comes to cooking and housework so I was surprised one year when, instead of throwing it away, she put the carcass from the Christmas turkey in her larder, saying she was going to use it to make soup. When I went to visit her three months later, however, the carcass was still there, completely covered in a thin layer of mould.

(Rhona)

When my daughter comes over for a meal, she washes her plate and cutlery – before I serve up the food. That's how much faith she has in my housekeeping abilities.

(Bev)

"Out, damned spot! Out, I say!"

(Well-known Scottish personality, Lady Macbeth, demonstrating her attitude to housework in Shakespeare's famous play)

When I told my mother I was going to stop smoking, she looked concerned and said: "A friend of mine stopped smoking and put on a lot of weight. I hope that doesn't happen to you."

(Madge)

Bear in mind this was over 30 years ago but I used to have the odd cigarette while bottle feeding my first baby and when, on one occasion, the main body of the cigarette separated from the tip while I was smoking it, I fired off an indignant letter of complaint to the manufacturers, pointing out that my infant son could have been injured as a result of their faulty merchandise. I got a letter of apology by return, plus a replacement pack of fags, and a voucher for another pack.

(Deirdrie)

When I was breast feeding my children in the middle of the night, I'd have a cigarette. It was the only way I could keep awake.

(Irene)

Packs of Kensitas cigarettes used to come with vouchers in them, that you could save up and exchange for gifts from their catalogue. My mum who was a heavy smoker, got me and my sister matching kilts from the catalogue, and a sun lounger for the garden which our neighbours probably thought was a bit pretentious as we lived in darkest Lanarkshire, near the steel works.

(Eve)

I've never smoked but my mum did, before she got lung cancer, and she used to reminisce about going out with her girlfriends to the dancing at the weekend, when they'd chip in for a pack of Sobranie Cocktail cigarettes – the ones in pastel colours with the gold tips – and they'd each smoke the cigarette that was the closest match to the colour of dress they were wearing.

(Beth)

When my husband's father died, I hired a mini bus to take us and other family members to the funeral. On the way to the church, one of his aunties made the driver pull up outside a shop so she could go in and buy cigarettes - despite the fact that my husband was due to help carry the coffin in.

(Audrey)

Annie (the author's late mum-in-law) and her drinking pal, Nan.

The fabulous busking piper,
Kristina MacDonald.

Tattooed bride and bridesmaids.

Musician Clare Robertson

Stylish, jewellery-loving Jeanette

Mrs. Bakshi and her fabulous
daughters, all born in Scotland
(apart from Neelam, left, who
strictly speaking, wasn't actually).

Emma Wong who, like all her friends in the picture, is SBC (Scottish born Chinese).

Gallus members of the Tartan Army

Wee Jimmy Krankie

Piper doll at the Museum of
Childhood, Edinburgh.

The first time I had my heart broken was when I was 11 and overheard my mum telling a friend how she and my dad used to write little notes in tiny writing and leave them for me, on the mantlepiece, with a 50 pence coin, from the Tooth Fairy. What my mother didn't realise was that, until that moment, I still believed it *was* a fairy that had written the notes and left the money for my teeth. I know it seems strange but it's not like you discuss fairies with your friends. You find out about things like Santa but not the Tooth Fairy. I cried my eyes out over that but I never told her.

(Maggie)

My husband left soon after our son was born but I was determined that he would have everything that children with two parents had. He never missed out at Christmas time but I told him that, even though Santa decided what presents he was going to get – based on his behaviour over the year – and then delivered them, he sent me a bill a few months later and I had to go out to work to pay for them!

(Lynn)

I'd been in the jail for five months for burglary and when I came out, my wife told me she was pregnant. We already had three kids and I thought, fair enough. But you work it out: I'd been in jail five months and the baby wasn't born until six months after I got out. When I started asking questions, she admitted that the man she'd got in to decorate the house had done more than paper and paint the walls. To be honest, I never felt the same about that wean as I did the others.

(Norrie)

I'ver never been a jealous person so when I discovered that the married woman my new husband was having an affair with was pregnant – and in no position to keep the baby – I said we'd take it. I've never regretted the decision and never felt less love for my son than for my biological daughter. My husband was another matter. We eventually divorced when I found out he'd started another family up in Aberdeen! But we've all kept in touch over the years.

(Janice)

I was 17 and at a family Hogmanay party, doing the Samba with my aunt, when she suddenly pointed across the room and said: "See than man over there?" "Aye" I said "that's my faither." "No" she said back "that's not your faither. Your real faither is . . . " and she named a man I'd never heard of. When I confronted my mother, she admitted she'd had an affair with a soldier who had been billeted with them before he went off to war. He and I met up once when I was in my 30s but it didn't go well. I sometimes wonder if my mother would ever have told me the truth, if my aunt hadn't spilled the beans.

(Andy)

My husband was married for a short time in his early 20s and hadn't seen his ex-wife for years – until he spotted her in a pub when we were having a night out. He must have been staring at her a bit too intensely because she came stalking over, quite aggressively, and said: "Sorry – do I know you?" And he replied: "Well, you should do – you used to be married to me."

(Fiona)

A neighbour, a former nurse, who had heard I was being treated for cancer came up to me in the street and asked how I was. Feeling very upbeat that day, I told her that things were going well and that staff at the hospital had been really great. "Oh aye" she said "they're always extra nice to the worst cases."

(Nan)

When I brought my German girlfriend home for dinner for the first time, my gran who was in her 80s, watched as she discarded the green tops from each of the strawberries she was going to eat, taking a small part of the fruit with it. After a few moments my gran said: "They would have eaten those bits in the concentration camps, you know." This was followed by a dead silence, not surprisingly.

(Peter)

This was years ago. I was flying into Glasgow airport, bringing my new Australian husband with me to meet the family for the first time, and we were on the same flight from London that Lulu was on. My mum was trying to catch a glimpse of us coming off the plane but reporters and photographers were blocking her view. So she asked a woman standing next to her what all the fuss was about and she replies: "Lulu's coming off this plane." My mum says back to her: "Lulu? Who cares about her? My lassie's coming from Austrialia with her new man! I'll bet Lulu's mother isn't even here!" And the wee wumman says: " I *am* her mother."

(from an internet forum)

I noticed two women looking at a dead pigeon lying on the pavement which had apparently met a somewhat violent end, as its head was almost severed from its body. They tutted over it for a few moments but as they moved off, one of them said to the other: "Mind you, I can think of worse ways to die."

(Greta)

I was buying myself a cheap watch and when I remarked to the sales girl that the one I had chosen claimed to be water resistant, she said: "Aye - but don't breath on it."

(Jan)

A driving examiner seeking £15,000 damages for whiplash has described the Edinburgh woman who he claims caused the injury as "the worst learner driver" he had ever had at the wheel. During her test, which she failed, he had recorded 14 faults - five of them serious and one dangerous.

(from a news report)

A mother-of-two from Clackmannanshire stabbed her partner to death after a row about music, a court heard yesterday. The woman admitted culpable homicide but claimed her partner had tried to throw a television set at her before she attacked him with a kitchen knife.

(from a news report)

A woman who said she had been trying to get pregnant "for several years", told a court in Glasgow that her two miscarriages had come about as a result of the Maryhill drug dealer who was on trial 'spiking' her heroin.

(from a news report)

This young, slim blond woman with her hair in a pony tail came into the shop one day. She was quite attractive but the main reason I noticed her was that she only had one leg and was on crutches. After a short while, it became apparent that she had come in to shoplift so she was escorted off the premises and told not to come back. But only a few days later, the same woman reappeared and when she was reminded that she had been barred, she said: "You must have me mixed up with someone else."

(James)

"We were up seeing Tracey in Greenock and we took the 'wee man' along; he's 15 months and she's pregnant again. Noo we're visiting my son in Kilmarnock. It's a day oot, really. You get sandwiches and everything. It's great!"

(Woman on the train, talking about visiting her children in prison.)

"I didn't know I had to be in the f*****' court for half eleven! My drugs support worker never told me."

(Woman on a Clydebank bus)

My sister had been away getting treatment for her drug addiction and when she came to see me after she got out, she wasn't speaking properly and I said: "Why have you not got your teeth in?" and she said: "I lost them in rehab."

(Caitlin)

A plush hairdressing awards ceremony in Glasgow descended into chaos when police were called after a female guest was allegedly head butted by another woman and violent scenes erupted. Witnesses reported that someone was struck with a handbag, a woman exposed her backside to the audience and Miss Scotland, who was a VIP guest at the event, had her crown knocked off.

(from a news report)

I went along to this
boxing gym in Renfrew
and when the guy there
asked me why I was
attracted to the sport I
said: "I want to hit
people."

(young woman boxer being interviewed
on Radio Scotland)

"I still go to the pub and have a drink with my friends" she says. "But I wouldn't get moroculous now." *Moroculous?* "You know - like being sick against a wall or something."

(Mhairi Black, being interviewed by an English journalist on how her life has changed since becoming the UK's youngest MP.)

"You smell of wine."

What Andy Murray said to his mum, Judy when she crashed his U.S. Open press conference in 2012, bringing Sean Connery and Sir Alex Ferguson along with her.

My mum's a really nice person but she's an alcoholic. She told my dad she was stopping but she was putting her drink in a Cillit Bang bottle so if he came in unexpectedly, she could pretend she was doing the house work. I brought my boyfriend home one day and he came rushing into the kitchen looking really upset and said: "Your mum's in the living room drinking Cillit Bang!" and I said: "Don't worry - it's cider."

(Audrey)

A former pub owner celebrated her 100th birthday - by having the first alcoholic drink of her life. Annie Mackie, who lived through two world wars and has outlived three of her four children and both husbands, raised a glass of sherry after a century of staying sober. Despite the long-anticipated wait, Annie from Aberdeenshire, said she didn't like the sherry very much and only had a tiny sip.

(from a news report)

The G.P. nurse had a big smile on her face when she told me I was pregnant with my first baby. "So - what's your reaction to the news?" she asked. "A bit disappointed" I replied "if it means I'll have to cancel the skiing holiday I booked last month."

(Viv)

I was a change-of-life baby. My mother had what she thought was her last child - baby number six - nine years before I was born. So I never got the impression that I was wanted. But I went to a fortune teller recently who told me: "Your mum wants you to know that she's proud of you." So that was nice to hear.

(Marilyn)

When I remarked to another mum that I was finding it hard to get my baby daughter up and ready in time to walk my older child to school in the morning, she said: "Why bother taking the baby with you? If she's asleep, leave her at home. That's what I used to do." Horrified, I asked what would happen if there was a fire. "I always left the front door unlocked" she replied "so the emergency services wouldn't have to break it down."

(Ruth)

I used to get my two boys to behave by telling them that, if they ran off when we were on a day out, they'd get kidnapped. It was the only thing that worked with them.

(Helen)

My mother used to
punch me on the
muscle on my arm,
for what she called
"dumb insolence."

(Stephen)

My mum would give me and my brother an occasional clout, for no reason, and if you asked what was that for, she'd say: *"that's for nothin' - see what you get for somethin'."*

(comedian Alan Cochrane talking about his Scottish mother)

A drunk childminder from Inverness injured a 13-year-old boy in her care by stabbing him after he refused to stop playing computer games, a court has heard. The woman, 55, lunged at the boy with a kitchen knife after they rowed about his continued use of an Xbox console.

(from a news report)

Why did I end up getting most of my education in "List D" schools? Because my mother used to send me out shop lifting and breaking into people's houses - that's why.

(Stewart)

"anyone else's mum come & talk to you while your in the bath & then her pal comes along as well? just mines then"

(a Scottish tweeter)

My daughter was in P3 and I was reading through her "Home Diary" at a Parents' Night, waiting to speak to the teacher about how wonderful my child was. However, when I came across an entry which claimed that I had, apparently, gone out one night and hadn't come back until the following morning - with red and yellow paint on my bum! - I decided not to hang around. When I asked my daughter what on earth she had been playing at, she said she was bored writing the same old thing and had decided to make something up. "But didn't your teacher say anything?" I asked. "Just that 'bum' was a rude word and I should have used 'bottom' instead" she replied.

(Trish)

I run my own tattoo studio in Dundee and when I went to collect my daughter from nursery one day, they told me she'd been drawing tattoo-style designs on other girls' tights.

(Heather Dewar)

There were four girls in the family and it was my big sister's job to look after us when we got in from school until our mother came home from work. One day, she decided to give our mum a surprise and take us down to meet her off the bus. But it was freezing out, so she improvised ear muffs for the three of us, using sanitary towels which, in those days, were really thick and had a string loop at each end. You should have seen my mum's face when she saw us waiting at the bus stop with the Dr. White's on our heads and the string loops fixed around our ears!

(Maureen)

"Got shouted at by daughter no 1 this morning for having the temerity to speak to her just as she had the perfect selfie face!"

(a Scottish dad on Facebook)

My mother died and I was sent to live in Dundee with relatives, visiting my father in Glasgow during the holidays. When he married again, my school friends predicted his new wife would be like the wicked stepmothers in fairy tales. In fact, she was very nice and also rather glamorous, with blond hair, make up and fashionable clothes. I was able to tell my friends: "She's lovely - *and* she looks like Marilyn Monroe."

(Caryl)

When my fringe gets really long my mum alway says to me: *"You're like a coo lookin' through mist!"*

(Pauline)

Not being content, in my youth, with my less than curly hair, I would get my mum to do a home perm. On completion, she would always say: *"One more wave and you'd drown."*

(Jackie Henderson)

The first woman I ever saw with a tattoo was my grannie. She was born in 1900 and when she was a teenager, during WW1, she and some pals went to the cinema and scratched their initials onto the insides of their wrists and rubbed them with ink.

(John McNeillie, Scottish tattooer)

A Spanish visitor in the 15th century described Scottish women as being exceedingly courteous and honest. *"They are very graceful and handsome"* he wrote *"and dress much better than Englishwomen."*

I was in my 50s and had bought myself a pair of what I thought were really trendy, stripey, sailor-style trousers. On first wearing, I passed two teenage girls in Argyle Street who took in what I had on in a split second glance and remarked, as they walked by: "Shiver me timbers." I never wore the trousers again.

(Grace)

"What do you think of your new nylon nightie, Jenny?"

"I don't like it, May - I can see my semmit through it."

(Author Margaret Thomson Davis recalling a conversation she overhead on a bus, in the 1960s, between two women who had recently bougtht themselves nylon nighties, after years of wearing flannelette ones.)

I was taken into hospital for an emergency operation recently and I was thankful that they managed to sort out the problem using a local anaesthetic. Not because, at the age of 75, it would have taken me longer to recover from a general one, but I'd just had a pedicure and, for a general, they would have had to remove my lovely black toenail varnish.

(Lois)

"I'd like to apologise to the many shoe shop staff in Glasgow who have become caught up in my seemingly never ending quest for boots. You can stand down now, ladies. Following the serving of an Asbo, I've now been banned from every shoe emporium in the city."

(Journalist Alison Rowat)

Whenever my grannie was going out, she'd take her specs off, wash her face, then apply what she called "a wee dab of powder" to each cheek from her powder compact. It was the only make up she ever wore.

(Eileen)

Back in the early 1960s, you would never dream of wheeling your pram around the Botanic Gardens in the West End of Glasgow without your white gloves on.

(Joyce)

"Mum's giving me a lift up town after getting her tan done, looks like I'm being driven about by a 5 foot tall jobby"

(a Scottish tweeter)

A red-haired Scottish teenager who airline staff thought must be ill because she looked so pale, was eventually allowed to board a holiday flight with her family after being given the all clear by an airport paramedic. Said the father of the 14-year-old girl: "I told them: she is not sick. We live in Scotland. She is a red head and has a pale complexion. That's just the way she is."

(from a news report)

In the small Lanarkshire town I grew up in during the 1950s, old widow women dressed all in black. And there was one who would sit out on a seat in her front garden in good weather and cackle when I went past, exposing a single, brown-stained tooth.

(Richard)

A delighted Scots mum is returning home queen of the world – at knitting. Hazel Tindall is celebrating after clinching the world speed knitting title for the second time. The 55-year-old, from Shetland, pipped competitors from all over the globe to snatch glory at the tournament in America. And she had to keep her nerve in front of a crowd of more than 50,000 who watched as Hazel won with an amazing 262 stitches in three minutes.

(from a news report)

My mother was so Scottish she was known to put her finger on the ball during televised England-Scotland games to pull it back into the England half. It never worked, alas.

(Edwin Moore in "Scotland - 1000 things you need to know.")

There had been a bit of worry about the cost of repairs to the family home and that was maybe on her mind when, in the last weeks of her life, my elderly mum whose memory had been failing for some time, called me and my sister to her bedside and assured us that there was no need for us to worry about money because: "We have diamond mines . . . and a chocolate factory."

(Jean)

THE WEE GUIDE TO
« SCOTTISH WOMEN »

Mrs. Elizabeth Somerville (nee Elizabeth "Bessy" Watson) was born in Edinburgh in 1900. She had an amazing life. She played the pipes from when she was seven and, aged nine, she became the youngest suffragette in Scotland.

(from an essay by Edinburgh school pupil, Rosslyn Cole)

When my dad was born, his sister who was less than three at the time, was sent away for a few weeks to Fife to stay with her granny who lavished her with love and attention, much to the annoyance of two of her daughters who still lived at home and accused their mother of spoiling her. "Well, if she lives to my age" she told them "she'll have shed enough tears to wash away any amount of spoiling."

(Val)

Sir Alex Ferguson has returned to his home city of Glasgow to support a campaign, led by former MP Maria Fyfe, to erect a statue in honour of social reformer Mary Barbour. Mary, who like Sir Alex came from Govan, led the Glasgow rent strikes of 1915, which forced a change in the law to curtail profiteering landlords. She's widely regarded as one of the most important social reformers of the last century. Glasgow currently has only three statues commemorating women.

(from a news report)

"Finally, to the five Scottish women who poured love into me: my great aunts May, Mary and Cissy, my grandmother Flora and my mother Anne. This is for you."

(Actress Julianne Moore accepting her Bafta Best Actress award.)

"Let's support each other, sisters - there's still a lot of work to be done!"

(Speaker, STUC women's conference.)

And now for a few
pages about dolls
and teddies . . .

I think dolls can be quite important when you're growing up, in terms of pushing the boundaries a bit when you're trying to make sense of the world around you. I had a Tiny Tears and then Cindy dolls and I used to experiment with them: trying on different outfits, styling and cutting their hair; putting them in a pram, wheeling it to the top of a hill and then letting it go, to see what would happen.

(Sharon)

I must have been five when I had my appendix taken out. That was in the days when children in hospital were tied to their beds, to stop them from falling out, and parents could only visit twice a week. I was miserable and would hardly talk to mine when they came to see me. Hoping to cheer me up, they offered to bring in my favourite doll to keep me company. But I didn't hesitate a moment before telling them: "No – Jennifer wouldn't like it here."

(Olive)

All my dolls' arms were
covered in tiny biro jags
where I had given them
pretend inoculations, like
being at the doctor's.

(Claire)

I had a very large doll, around three feet tall, with pink fluffy hair, and what I remember most about Audrey was that my mother used to wash *and* iron her clothes - including her underwear!

(Monica)

I wasn't a doll person - I had teddies. In fact, I can remember being quite sniffy when someone gave me a doll. I was moving house several years ago and had packed all my old teddies into a box and when the removal man saw what was in it he said: "Are the bears going too?" I said: "Of course!" They haven't come out of the box yet but I can't get rid of them. My sister had bears, too and she said: "You can't get rid of your teddies - they're the friends you had in childhood." I still buy my sister a small bear, when life is a bit hard and she needs a lift.

(Valerie)

I'm 81 but I still remember the time my sister gave my teddy away to a girl called Julie who lived in the next close. It wasn't long after the war and Julie's father was away in the army so I think my sister felt sorry for her. But times weren't that hard and surely she had toys of her own? My sister was eight and I was about 14 which is why I was too embarrassed to go and ask for it back. But I'd had it since I was a baby! It took me a long time to forgive her.

(Marlene)

I get my teddy
bear a stocking at
Christmas - and I
send him birthday
cards.

(Moira, aged 35)

About Deedee Cuddihy

Deedee Cuddihy is a journalist who was born and brought up in New York but has lived in Glasgow since the "Big Storm" of 1967 (which she slept through). Or was it 1968? After finishing art school in Glasgow, she realised being an artist would be too difficult - and being an art teacher would be even more difficult. So she became a journalist and has been one ever since. She is married to a Scotsman and has two grown up children - plus three granddaughters. "The Wee Guide to Scottish Women" is the eleventh in her Funny Scottish Books series, the other titles including the best-selling "How to Murder a Haggis" and "I Love Irn-Bru". *(The author would like to have been born Scottish but, as Joe E. Brown says in the film Some Like It Hot: "Well, nobody's perfect.")*